GW01237632

Starting
Secondary School

by
Marie-Thérèse Bougard

First published 2002
exclusively for WHSmith by

Hodder & Stoughton Educational
338 Euston Road
London
NW1 3BH

Illustrations © Hodder & Stoughton Educational 2002

All rights reserved. No part of this publication may be reproduced or
transmitted in any form or by any means, electronic or mechanical, including
photocopying, recording or any information storage and retrieval system,
without permission in writing from the publisher.

A CIP record for this book is available from the British Library.

Text: © 2002 Marie-Thérèse Bougard

Illustrator: Tony Linsell

Typeset by Fakenham Photosetting Ltd, Fakenham, Norfolk.

ISBN 0 340 84734 4

Printed and bound in Spain by Graphycems.

Contents

Introduction

The move from primary to secondary school can be quite an overwhelming experience. You will encounter completely new subject areas and a whole range of new topics and concepts, as well as new teachers and a new and much bigger school environment. Some people say it is like changing from a big fish in a small pond (primary school) into a small fish in a big pond (secondary school)!

The books in this *Starting Secondary School* series will help bridge the gap between primary and secondary school and ease the transition between the two.

From a big fish in a small pond to a small fish in a big pond.

This introduction will answer some of the most frequently asked questions about starting secondary school.

What are lessons like at secondary school?

You'll probably be placed in a tutor group, which meets for registration each day with the same teacher, and you are likely to stay with this group for quite a few subjects. In some subjects, like English and maths, you may be placed in a set with other children of similar ability to make it easier for you and the rest to work at a similar pace.

The timetable is very important at secondary school. Lessons are for set times and there may be a bell signalling the end of each lesson. Different subjects are taught in different rooms and you will be told and shown where to go. It is important to get to know your timetable as quickly as possible and to know where to go for each lesson. You could fill in the blank timetable at the end of this book to help you.

Will I be able to find my way around?

Life at secondary school may seem very different to life at primary school at first. For a start, everything seems much bigger. The buildings are bigger, the students are bigger – and there are more of them! A common fear is of getting lost or not being able to find your way around. Don't worry. Your teachers will make sure you know where to go and there's always someone you can ask. Remember – if in doubt about anything, ask! Nobody will mind if you do. Everyone at the school is there to help you, and to help you to do your best.

How do secondary schools work?

Each subject follows a scheme of work, which has been agreed by each subject department and will be based on Key Stage 3 of the National Curriculum. You will mostly study the same subjects you did at primary school. The main difference is that you will have different teachers to help you. You will also begin to study at least one modern foreign language, usually French or German. The choice of languages available differs from school to school.

What about tests?

It is likely that you will have more tests and assessments at secondary school than you did at primary school. You will usually be told when these are to take place and will be given plenty of time to revise and prepare for them. If you are sensible and do your homework, these tests should not worry you at all.

What about homework?

Homework is set in accordance with an agreed timetable so that you will have different subjects to deal with on different evenings. In your first year this will not be too time-consuming. A good tip is to do your homework as soon as you can, rather than leave it till the last minute and rush it. And remember to take it to school with you on the day you are supposed to hand it in!

How will I cope with the extra freedom that I will have at secondary school?

A lot of emphasis is placed on being independent and responsible in secondary school. Thinking ahead and being organised will help you a lot. Always get to your lessons and take everything you need with you. The teachers will tell you what you need to bring to each lesson.

How will my parents know what I am doing at school?

Most schools use a homework diary in which homework is recorded and some schools ask parents to sign these regularly to show that they have read them. It is important that your parents know what your are doing at school. This is one way of helping them find out. Don't forget to talk to them too! Your school will probably also have regular open evenings when your parents will be invited to school to talk to your teachers and discuss your progress.

How will this book help me?

Introduction

This book contains many activities to help you revise basic French. It is divided into six main units:

présentations

This unit revises basic language such as yes and no, simple greetings and introductions, as well as numbers up to 12.

chez moi

This unit revises language used to talk about different countries, your home, your family and pets.

j'aime

This unit revises language used to talk about food and drink, friends and hobbies, as well as numbers up to 30.

cinq

le look

This unit revises language such as colours, the body, clothes and simple descriptions of people.

l'école

This unit revises the names of school subjects, days of the week and the time, as well as numbers up to 69.

l'année

This unit revises the names of the months and seasons, phrases to do with the weather, birthdays and holidays, as well as numbers up to 100.

What's in each unit?

Each of the six units is made of four or five self-contained spreads. Each spread has activities for you to do: simple cartoons to read, crosswords, wordsearches, quizzes, games and puzzles.

Each spread has two sections to help you with the language:

mini-dico

'Dico' is slang for 'dictionnaire', the French word for 'dictionary'. This section lists all the new words and expressions used on that spread.

bons points

'Bons points' can mean either 'good points' or 'good marks'. With arrows pointing at various words and phrases, this section provides helpful hints for good pronunciation as well as simple grammar explanations.

The following section appears on most spreads:

par cœur

'Par cœur' means 'by heart' and it is recommended you learn its contents by heart.
In most cases it includes made-up rhymes to help you remember useful vocabulary and concentrate on good pronunciation.
Some of these sections refer to **moi... moi... moi...** (see page 7), and you are encouraged to write simple sentences about yourself and learn them by heart. It will help build your confidence so you can have simple conversations in French about things that matter to you.

Most units include at least one of the following sections:

mots croisés

This is French for 'crossword', and these grids will help you revise key vocabulary.

moi... moi... moi...

'Moi' means 'me'. This section is for you to illustrate with your own drawings or photographs, and fill in with details about your own life.

pour jouer

'Jouer' means 'to play'. This section includes simple board games for you to play with a friend. You will need dice and counters for these.

pour chanter

'Chanter' means 'to sing'. There are three songs included in this book. The lyrics of the first two were specially written for you to revise and remember key language. The third one is an existing Christmas song that uses a lot of words you will already be familiar with. All three songs are to traditional tunes, and the music scores have been included – you may find them useful if you play the piano, keyboard, flute or recorder.

You will also find two sections called **sondage.**
'Sondage' means 'opinion poll'. These sections use basic vocabulary, such as colours or qualities, as a starting point. You will be asked to state your own preferences and ask a friend or two to do the same, and then compare the results.

Enjoy your workbook!
Amuse-toi bien!

sept

présentations

bons points

- Pronounce '**salut**' as if there is no 't' at the end.

- Say your 'r's from the back of the throat.

- '**Ça va**' can be used either as a question meaning 'How are you?' or as a reply meaning 'I'm fine'.

1 salut!

Read the cartoon story, and find the French for:

1 hi   ....
2 yes   ....
3 no   ....
4 help   ....
5 thank you   ....
6 are you OK? ....
7 I'm OK   ....
8 and you?   ....

huit

Choose the right label for each bubble.

au secours!   merci

salut!   ça va?

1

2

3

4

au secours	help
ça va	I'm fine/OK
ça va?	how are you?/
	are you OK?
et toi?	and you?
merci	thank you
non	no
oui	yes
salut	hi

par cœur

Learn this by heart.

Salut, Lulu!
Ça va, Sarah?
Merci, Henri.

neuf

présentations

bons points

- Do not pronounce the final 'd' of 'Edouard'.

- 'Bonsoir', 'au revoir', 'Omar' and 'Edouard' rhyme: they all end with the same 'ar' sound.

- Do not pronounce the 't' of 'nuit'. 'Nuit' rhymes with 'Annie'.

2 au revoir!

Look at the cartoons, and find the French for:

1 goodbye   ....
2 good evening   ....
3 good morning   ....
4 good night   ....
5 please   ....

Bonjour!

Bonsoir!

Bonne nuit!

S'il te plaît!

Au revoir

Insert all the missing vowels.

mini-dico

au revoir — goodbye

bonjour — good morning, hello

bonne nuit — good night

bonsoir — good evening

s'il te plaît — please

par cœur

Learn this by heart.

Bonsoir, Omar!

Au revoir, Edouard!

Bonne nuit, Annie!

présentations

bons points

- Say '**deux**' as if there is no 'x' at the end.

- Say '**trois**' as if there is no 's' at the end.

- '**Six**' and '**dix**' both sound as if the 'x' is a double 's'.

3 les numéros

mots croisés

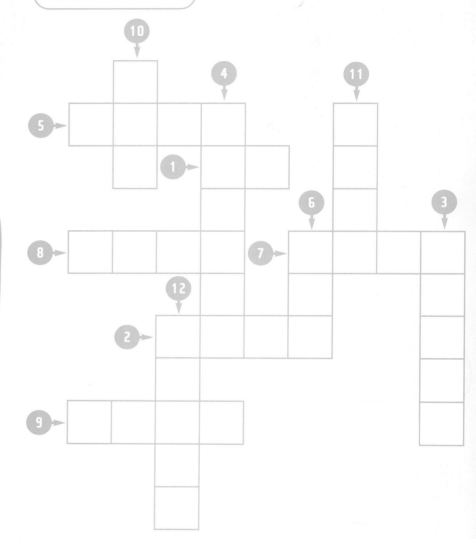

Which number rhymes with which name?

2 – deux	Alice
3 – trois	Annette
6 – six	François
7 – sept	Madame Ventouse
9 – neuf	Matthieu
12 – douze	Monsieur Lebœuf

douze

Join the dots to find out what Milou is doing.

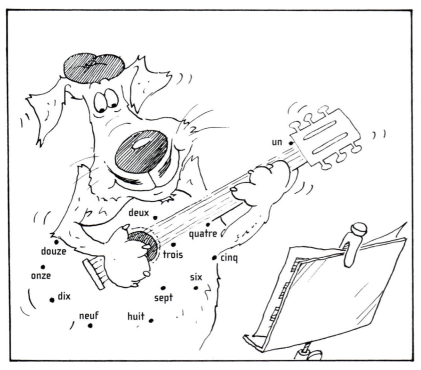

un	1
deux	2
trois	3
quatre	4
cinq	5
six	6
sept	7
huit	8
neuf	9
dix	10
onze	11
douze	12

par cœur

Learn this by heart.

1, 2, 3, François!

4, 5, 6, Alice!

7, 8, 9, Monsieur Lebœuf!

10, 11, 12, Madame Ventouse!

treize

présentations

- '**Tu as quel âge?**', the French way of saying 'How old are you?' means – literally – 'What age do you have?'

- That is the reason why the answer starts with '**J'ai...**' 'which is the way of saying of 'I have'.

J'ai onze ans

4 tu t'appelles comment?

Read the cartoon story, and find the French for:

1 How old are you?   ....
2 What's your name?   ....
3 My name is...   ....

It's the first day at a new school. Alex, Julie and Sam are nervous – they don't know anybody ...

COLLÈGE

Tu t'appelles comment?

Je m'appelle Julie. Et toi?

Je m'appelle Alex.

Tu as quel âge?

J'ai dix ans. Et toi?

J'ai onze ans.

Tu t'appelles comment?

Je m'appelle Sam. Et toi?

Je m'appelle Julie.

Au revoir!

Salut!

COLLÈGE

Tu as quel âge?

J'ai douze ans? Et toi?

J'ai onze ans.

Au revoir!

Who is the youngest? Alex, Julie or Sam?   ....
Who is the oldest? Alex, Julie or Sam?   ....

quatorze

moi... moi... moi...

Stick a picture of yourself (or draw one) in the space and complete
the speech bubble with information about your name and your age.

Bonjour! Je m'appelle

.... *scruan*

J'ai .... *huit* .... ans.

mini-dico

j'ai ... ans
I'm ... years old

je m'appelle ...
my name's ...

Tu as quel âge?
How old are you?

Tu t'appelles comment?
What's your name?

par cœur

When you have completed the speech bubble, learn it by heart.

chez moi

- When saying where you live, introduce the town or city with '**à**'.

- Most names of countries are introduced with '**en**', but there are exceptions: '**le Canada**' and '**le pays de Galles**' are introduced with '**au**'. '**les USA**' is introduced with '**aux**'.

5 tu habites où?

Look at the speech bubbles
and match each town with the correct country.

Aberystwyth ...	est aux USA.
Birmingham ...	est en Suisse.
Bruxelles ...	est en Ecosse.
Glasgow ...	est en France.
Chicago ...	est en Irlande.
Québec ...	est au Canada.
Genève ...	est en Belgique.
Dublin ...	est en Angleterre.
Paris ...	est au pays de Galles

CONGRÈS DES APPRENTIS SORCIERS

Tu habites où?

J'habite à Birmingham ... en Angleterre. Et toi?

Moi, j'habite au pays de Galles ... à Aberystwyth.

J'habite aux USA ... à Chicago. Et toi?

J'habite en France. J'habite à Paris. Et toi?

J'habite en Suisse ... à Genève.

Et toi? Tu habites où?

J'habite en Ecosse ... à Glasgow.

J'habite en Belgique ... à Bruxelles.

J'habite au Canada ... à Québec. Et toi?

J'habite en Irlande ... à Dublin.

mots croisés

mini-dico

Horizontalement ▶

2 New York est aux ___

3 Glasgow est en _____

6 Dublin est en _____

9 Manchester est en _____

10 Québec est au _____

Verticalement ▼

1 Aberystwyth est au pays de _____

4 Genève est en _____

5 Bruxelles est en _____

7 Cardiff est au _____ de Galles

8 Calais est en _____

l'Angleterre	England
la Belgique	Belgium
le Canada	Canada
l'Ecosse	Scotland
la France	France
l'Irlande	Ireland
le pays de Galles	Wales
la Suisse	Switzerland
les USA	the USA
à	in
au(x)	in
en	in
est	is
j'habite	I live
tu habites où?	where do you live?

par cœur

Learn this by heart.

Tu habites où?
1, 2 3, au Canada?
4, 5, 6, en Suisse?
7, 8, 9, à Châteauneuf?
10, 11, 12,
j'habite à Toulouse.

dix-sept

chez moi

bons points

- 'Il y a' means both 'there is' and 'there are'.

- When talking about what's missing, use 'de' after 'il n'y a pas'.

- 'Salle de bains' rhymes with 'jardin'. Do not pronounce the 's' at the end of 'bains'.

- 'Toilettes' sounds quite different from 'toilet'. The first syllable sounds the same as 'toi' in 'et toi?' (see page 9). Do not pronounce the 's' at the end of the word.

Look at the picture for three minutes, then hide it and do the memory quiz below.

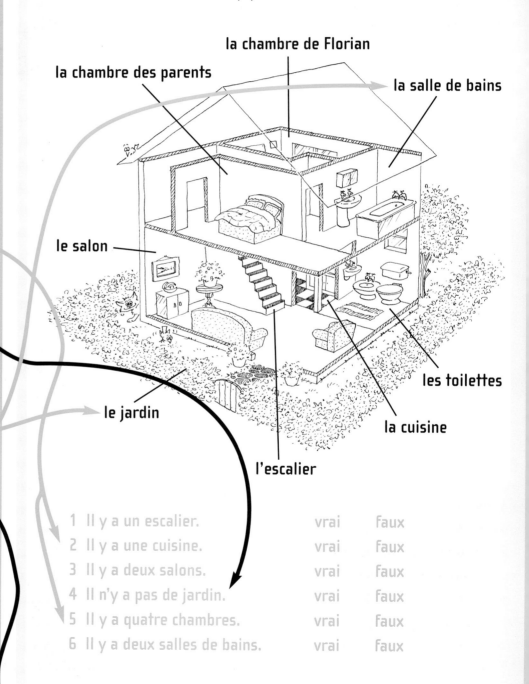

la chambre de Florian

la chambre des parents

la salle de bains

le salon

les toilettes

le jardin

la cuisine

l'escalier

1 Il y a un escalier.	vrai	faux
2 Il y a une cuisine.	vrai	faux
3 Il y a deux salons.	vrai	faux
4 Il n'y a pas de jardin.	vrai	faux
5 Il y a quatre chambres.	vrai	faux
6 Il y a deux salles de bains.	vrai	faux

dix-huit

Find in the grid the French for:

1 bedroom ....
2 garden ....
3 house ....
4 kitchen ....
5 sitting room ....
6 staircase ....
7 toilet ....

mini-dico

●	E	S	C	A	L	I	E	R
T	O	I	L	E	T	T	E	S
S	S	C	U	I	S	I	N	E
A	A	L	L	E	D	E	B	A
L	I	J	A	R	D	I	N	N
O	C	H	A	M	B	R	E	S
N	M	A	I	S	O	N	●	●

The remaining letters make up the name of another room. What is it?

....

la chambre	bedroom
la cuisine	kitchen
l'escalier	staircase
le jardin	garden
la salle de bains	bathroom
le salon	sitting room
les toilettes	toilet
faux	false
vrai	true
il y a . . .	there is/ are . . .
il n'y a pas de . . .	there is no . . .

par cœur

Learn this by heart.

A la maison,
Louison est dans le salon,
Karine est dans la cuisine.
Antoinette est aux toilettes
et Justin est dans le jardin.

dix-neuf

bons points

- To say 'Fabien's brother' or 'Fabien's sister' in French, you need to say 'the brother of Fabien' or 'the sister of Fabien'. The French for 'of' is '**de**'.

- The French for 'my' is '**mon**' when it is followed by a masculine word.

- The French for 'my' is '**ma**' when it is followed by a feminine word.

- The French for 'my' is '**mes**' when it is followed by a word in the plural.

7 ma famille

Look at the pictures of Fabien's family, and find the French for:

1 brother .... 6 grandmother ....
2 sister .... 7 stepfather ....
3 father .... 8 stepmother ....
4 mother .... 9 stepsister ....
5 grandfather ....

La famille de Fabien

Fabien

le frère de Fabien

le père de Fabien

la mère de Fabien

la belle-mère de Fabien

le beau-père de Fabien

le grand-père de Fabien

la grand-mère de Fabien

la sœur de Fabien

la demi-sœur de Fabien

vingt

Which picture fits the description? ....

Voici ma famille: mes grands-parents,
ma mère et mon beau-père,
mon frère (Pierre), ma demi-sœur (Océane)
et... moi (Thomas)!

mini-dico

le beau-père	stepfather
la belle-mère	stepmother
la demi-sœur	stepsister
le frère	brother
la grand-mère	grandmother
le grand-père	grandfather
les grands-parents	grandparents
la mère	mother
le père	father
la sœur	sister
de	of
ma	my
mes	my
mon	my
voici	here's

pour jouer

Use the family grid on page 20 to play with one or two friends.

You need one die and three counters, and a piece of paper and pen for each player.

Each player chooses three characters from the grid and writes their names on their sheet of paper. Player 1 places a counter on a blank box of their choice, casts the die and moves the counter accordingly. If the counter lands on a box with one of the characters he/she had chosen, Player 1 continues with the second counter. If not, it is the next player's turn.

You can move the counters:
from left to right ▶
from right to left ◀
from top to bottom ▼
from bottom to top ▲
But you cannot move diagonally.

The winner is the first person with all three counters on the correct boxes.

vingt et un

chez moi

bons points

- You need to pronounce 'un **éléphant**' as if it is spelt 'unnéléphan'. Do not pronounce the 't' at the end.

- You need to pronounce 'un **ours**' as if it is spelt 'un nours'. You need to pronounce the 's' at the end.

8 mes animaux

Which animals can you see in Diane's bedroom?

Dans la chambre de Diane, il y a …

1	un chat	oui	non
2	un ours	oui	non
3	un lapin	oui	non
4	un chien	oui	non
5	un cheval	oui	non
6	une girafe	oui	non
7	un serpent	oui	non
8	un poisson	oui	non
9	un hamster	oui	non
10	un éléphant	oui	non

vingt-deux

moi... moi... moi...

Stick down a picture of your family and/or your pets,
and complete the speech bubble.

> J'ai ....
>
> Je n'ai pas de
>
> ....

mini-dico

un chat	cat
un cheval	horse
un chien	dog
un éléphant	elephant
une girafe	giraffe
un hamster	hamster
un lapin	rabbit
un ours	bear
un poisson	fish
un serpent	snake

par cœur

When you have completed the speech bubble, learn it by heart.

9 bon appétit!

Find the right illustration for each item on the menu.

A B C D

E F G H

I J K L

Tu as faim?
- sandwich au fromage
- sandwich au jambon
- sandwich au poulet
- frites
- salade
- pizza aux champignons
- glace à la vanille
- glace à la fraise
- gâteau au chocolat

Tu as soif?
- eau minérale
- jus d'orange
- limonade

- 'Tu as faim?' means literally 'do you have hunger?'

- 'Tu as soif?' means literally 'do you have thirst?'

Choose what you would like from the menu and complete the speech bubbles.

> J'ai faim.
> ....
> s'il vous plaît.

> J'ai soif.
> ....
> s'il vous plaît.

mots croisés

Horizontalement ▶

1 un ___ d'orange, s'il vous plaît
4 un _____ au fromage ou au poulet?
6 j'ai ____: un sandwich, s'il vous plaît
9
10 une ___ minérale, s'il vous plaît
11

Verticalement ▼

2 j'ai ____: une eau minérale, s'il vous plaît
3 une glace à la fraise ou à la _____?
5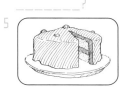
7 un sandwich au jambon ou au _____?
8 une _____ à la vanille ou à la fraise?

mini-dico

le champignon	mushroom
le chocolat	chocolate
l'eau minérale	mineral water
la fraise	strawberry
la frite	chip
le fromage	cheese
le gâteau	cake
la glace	ice cream
le jambon	ham
le jus d'orange	orange juice
la limonade	lemonade
la pizza	pizza
le poulet	chicken
la salade	salad
le sandwich	sandwich
la vanille	vanilla
j'ai faim	I'm hungry
j'ai soif	I'm thirsty
tu as faim?	are you hungry?
tu as soif?	are you thirsty?
bon appétit	enjoy your meal
s'il vous plaît	please

par cœur

When you have completed the speech bubbles on page 24, learn them by heart.

vingt-cinq

bons points

- Most French adjectives change depending on whether they are masculine or feminine.

- Most feminine adjectives need an extra 'e' at the end.

- The feminine of '**généreux**' is '**généreuse**'.

- The feminine of '**sportif**' is '**sportive**'.

- '**Sympa**' remains the same whether it is masculine or feminine.

10 mes copains

Read the bubbles to find out each person's name and write them down.

sondage

What's most important in a friend?
Number these qualities in order of importance to you,
then ask two friends and see if you agree.
(1 = most important; 7 = least important)

Le hit-parade des qualités			
	moi	1	2
cool			
calme			
sympa			
sportif/sportive			
marrant/marrante			
généreux/généreuse			
intelligent/intelligente			

mini-dico

mon copain	my (boy)friend
ma copine	my (girl)friend
bavard/bavarde	chatty
généreux/généreuse	generous
intelligent/intelligente	clever
marrant/marrante	funny
sportif/sportive	sporty
sympa	nice, friendly
s'appelle	is called
il est	he is
elle est	she is

par cœur

Learn this by heart.

Raoul est cool,
Malika est sympa,
Matthieu est généreux
Et Florian est marrant!

vingt-sept

bons points

- Pronounce 'natation' and 'équitation' as if they ended in 'ssion', and make them rhyme with 'non'.

- Do not say the 't' at the end of 'sport'. Pronounce the 'r' from the back of your throat.

11 le sport

Do this quiz and find out how sporty you are.

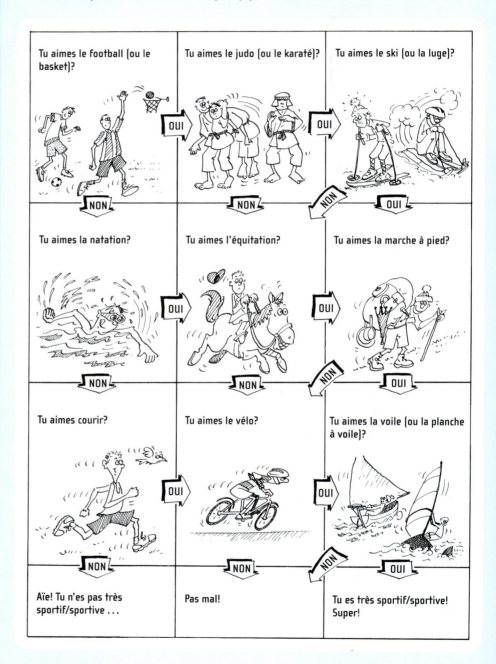

Complete the bubbles.

J'aime _____

J'aime _____

J'aime _____

J'aime _____

par cœur

Learn this by heart.

Le sport, d'accord!

La marche à pied et le karaté, OK!

La voile, géniale!

Mais le ski, non merci!

L'équitation, attention!

Et la natation, non, non, non!

le basket	basketball
courir	to run
l'équitation	horseriding
le football	football
le judo	judo
le karaté	karate
la luge	sledging
la marche à pied	
	walking
la natation	swimming
la planche à voile	
	windsurfing
le ski	skiing
le vélo	cycling
la voile	sailing
aïe	ouch!
d'accord	OK
génial/e	brilliant
pas mal	not bad
super	great
très	very

vingt-neuf

bons points

- Say 'quatorze' and 'quinze' as if they are spelt 'katorze' and 'kinze'. Don't pronounce the 'u'.

- Say 'vingt' as if it is spelt 'vin', but pronounce the 't' in 'vingt-deux', 'vingt-trois' etc.

12 récréation

How many numbers can you see in the grid?

T	R	E	I	Z	E	Q
Q	R	D	V	I	N	U
U	G	E	E	T	Q	A
I	U	N	N	U	U	T
N	A	T	R	T	X	O
Z	S	E	I	Z	E	R
E	V	I	N	G	T	Z
E	D	O	U	Z	E	E

The remaining letters make up another number. What is it?

....

Complete the series.

1 treize, seize, dix-neuf, vingt-deux, ...
2 vingt-huit, vingt-six, vingt-quatre, ...
3 dix, quinze, vingt, vingt-cinq, ...
4 dix-neuf, dix-sept, quinze, ...
5 quatorze, seize, dix-huit, ...
6 onze, quinze, ...

trente

pour chanter

You can sing this to the tune of 'Au clair de la lune'.

Je m'ap-pelle Ca- mi-lle, j'ha-bite à Mou-lins
Ma co- pine Pau- li-ne a- dore les pi- zzas.

A- vec ma fa- mi-lle: une sœur et trois chiens.
Elle aime la va- ni-lle et le cho-co- lat.

Ma sœur s'ap-pelle Li- ne, je n'ai pas de frère,
Elle est très spor -ti- ve, elle fait du ju- do

mais dans la cui- si- ne, il y a mon ham-ster.
a- vec A-man- di- ne et a- vec Thé- o.

Je m'appelle Camille
J'habite à Moulins
Avec ma famille
Une sœur et trois chiens.

Ma sœur s'appelle Line
Je n'ai pas de frère
Mais dans la cuisine
Il y a mon hamster.

Ma copine Pauline
Adore les pizzas.
Elle aime la vanille
Et le chocolat.

Elle est très sportive
Elle fait du judo
Avec Amandine
Et avec Théo.

trente et un

mini-dico

treize	13
quatorze	14
quinze	15
seize	16
dix-sept	17
dix-huit	18
dix-neuf	19
vingt	20
vingt et un	21
vingt-deux	22
vingt-trois	23
vingt-quatre	24
vingt-cinq	25
vingt-six	26
vingt-sept	27
vingt-huit	28
vingt-neuf	29
trente	30

bons points

- Here is a list of other hobbies to help you:

peindre – to paint

dessiner – to draw

faire du théâtre – to do drama

faire la cuisine – to cook

regarder la télé – to watch TV

jouer du piano – to play the piano

aller au cinéma – to go to the cinema

écouter la musique – to listen to music

13 mes passe-temps

Read the cartoon story and find the French for:
1 playing cards ....
2 computers ....
3 reading ....
4 dancing ....
5 I like that ....
6 I hate that ....

moi... moi... moi...

Stick in a picture illustrating your favourite hobbies.
Then complete the speech bubble
saying what you like doing in your spare time.

J'aime

....

....

mini-dico

la flûte	flute
l'ordinateur	computer
le passe-temps	hobby
j'aime ça	I like that
je déteste ça	I hate that
danser	to dance
jouer aux cartes	to play cards
jouer de la flûte	to play the flute
lire	to read

par cœur

When you have completed the speech bubble,
learn it by heart.

trente-trois

bons points

- 'Marron' doesn't mean 'maroon', it means 'brown'.

- The French for 'maroon' is 'bordeaux'.

14 mes couleurs préférées

Colour in each box according to the captions.

les trois couleurs primaires:

rouge	jaune	bleu

les couleurs complémentaires:

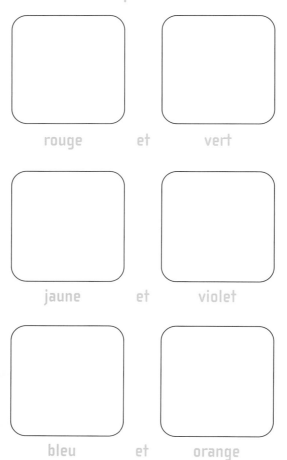

rouge et vert

jaune et violet

bleu et orange

sondage

Number each colour in order of preference, then ask two friends and see if you have similar tastes.
(1 = favourite; 12 = least favourite)

le hit-parade des couleurs			
	moi	1	2
bleu			
rouge			
jaune			
orange			
vert			
violet			
noir			
gris			
blanc			
rose			
bordeaux			
marron			

mini-dico

l'arc-en-ciel	rainbow
la couleur	colour
préféré	favourite
blanc	white
bleu	blue
bordeaux	maroon
gris	grey
indigo	indigo
jaune	yellow
marron	brown
noir	black
orange	orange
rose	pink
rouge	red
vert	green
violet	purple

par cœur

Draw a rainbow and learn this by heart.

Violet, indigo, bleu,
Vert, jaune,
Orange, rouge
C'est l'arc-en-ciel!

le look

- The French for 'hair' is always plural.
  Do not pronounce the 'x' at the end.

- Pronounce 'les yeux' as if it is spelt 'les zieu'.
  Do not pronounce the 'x' at the end.

15 le corps

Roméo le robot

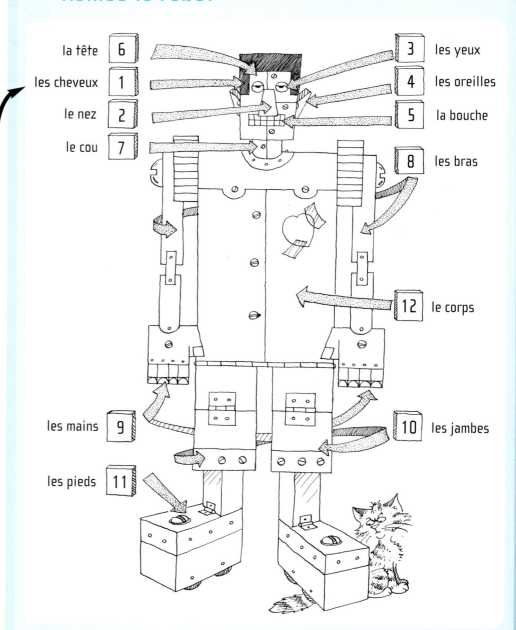

la tête [6]

les cheveux [1]

le nez [2]

le cou [7]

[3] les yeux

[4] les oreilles

[5] la bouche

[8] les bras

[12] le corps

les mains [9]

[10] les jambes

les pieds [11]

Look at Roméo le robot, and find the French for:

1 eyes ....
2 feet ....
3 hair ....
4 arms ....
5 nose ....
6 head ....
7 body ....
8 mouth ....

pour jouer

Use the picture on page 36 to play with one or two friends.

- You need two dice, and a piece of paper and pen for each player.
- Players take it in turn to throw one or two dice. To start, you need to throw a 12 or a 6. If you throw a 6, you can draw the head on your piece of paper. If you throw a 12, you can draw the body. Then you continue, drawing another part of the robot according to what number you have thrown.
- You cannot draw the hair, eyes, ears, nose or mouth if you haven't drawn the head.
- You cannot draw the arms, hands, legs and feet until you have drawn the body.
- You cannot draw the neck until you have drawn either the body or the head.
- The first player with a complete robot wins the game.

mini-dico

la bouche	mouth
le bras	arm
les cheveux	hair
le corps	body
le cou	neck
la jambe	leg
la main	hand
le nez	nose
l'oreille	ear
le pied	foot
la tête	head
les yeux	eyes

le look

bons points

- In French, '**le pantalon**' and '**le jean**' are singular – unless you are talking about more than one pair. In the same way, the French for 'pyjamas' is '**le pyjama**'.

- Say '**manteau**' and '**chapeau**' as if they are spelt 'manto' and 'chapo'.

16 mes vêtements préférés

Look at the clothes and add colours and patterns to suit your own taste and style.

Find the French for:

1 trousers .... 3 shoes ....

2 jacket .... 4 tie ....

Follow the description below to complete the picture of the prime suspect.

Le suspect porte un manteau bleu, un jean gris et des bottes marronnes. Il porte un chapeau rouge, une écharpe verte et des gants noirs.

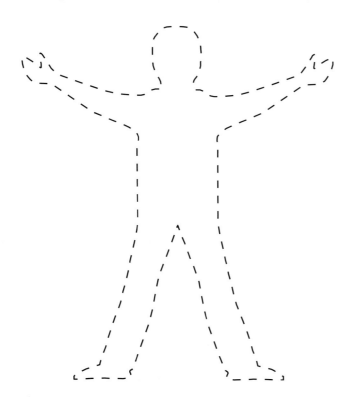

mini-dico

les baskets	trainers
le blouson	bomber jacket
les bottes	high boots
le chapeau	hat
les chausettes	socks
les chaussures	shoes
la chemise	shirt
le collant	tights
la cravate	tie
l'écharpe	scarf
les gants	gloves
le jean	jeans
la jupe	skirt
le manteau	winter coat
le pantalon	trousers
le pull	sweater
la robe	dress
le sweat	sweatshirt
le tee-shirt	t-shirt
la veste	jacket
les vêtements	clothes
porte	is wearing

par cœur

Learn this by heart.

J'aime la veste verte d'Yvette,
les gants blancs de Bertrand
et la cravate d'Agathe,
mais je déteste les chausettes violettes de Josette!

le look

- When describing a girl, you need to use the feminine form of adjectives, and say '**elle est petite**' or '**elle est grande**'.

- The feminine form of '**gros**' is slightly irregular: '**grosse**'.

- If you wear glasses, say '**je porte des lunettes**'.

- If you are neither tall nor small, say '**je suis de taille moyenne**'.

17 petit ou grand?

Read the cartoon story, and find the French for:

1 long hair ....
2 blue eyes ....
3 brown eyes ....
4 slim ....
5 tall ....
6 small ....

quarante

moi... moi... moi...

Stick in a picture of yourself and complete the description.

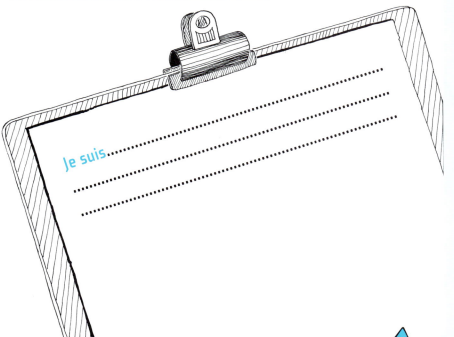

Je suis..
....
....

mini-dico

court/courte	short
grand/grande	tall
gros/grosse	fat
long/longue	long
mince	slim
petit/petite	small
elle a	she has
j'ai	I have
je suis	I am
tu as	you have
tu es	you are
c'est	it is
ce n'est pas	it is not
là	there

Je suis . . .

bons points

- Pronounce '**musique**' and '**informatique**' as if they end in 'ik'.

- Pronounce the 'r's in '**mardi**', '**mercredi**' and '**vendredi**' from the back of the throat.

- '**Sciences**' rhymes with '**Clémence**' – do not pronounce the 's' at the end.

- '**Sport**' rhymes with '**Nestor**' – do not pronounce the 't' at the end.

18 mes matières préférées

Put back all the missing vowels.

Find the right symbol for each school subject.

sport	français	musique
maths	histoire	géographie
anglais	sciences	informatique

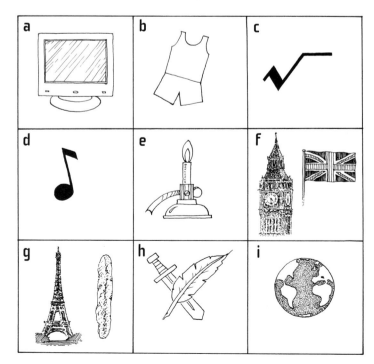

Read the bubbles and look at the timetable.
Is it Julien's or Samia's?

J'aime le mardi, parce que j'ai le sport et la musique. La prof de sport est très sympa et j'adore la musique: c'est ma matière préférée.

Je déteste le jeudi. J'ai l'anglais et la géographie. Je déteste la géographie et je n'aime pas le prof d'anglais.

mini-dico

l'école	school
l'anglais	English
le français	French
la géographie	geography
l'histoire	history
l'informatique	IT
les maths	maths
la matière	school subject
la musique	music
les sciences	science
le sport	PE
lundi	Monday
mardi	Tuesday
mercredi	Wednesday
jeudi	Thursday
vendredi	Friday
samedi	Saturday
dimanche	Sunday

	lundi	mardi	mercredi	jeudi	vendredi	samedi
8h–9h	français	maths		sciences		informatique
9h–10h	maths	maths		géographie	maths	anglais
			récréation			
10h15–11h15	dessin	français		français	anglais	sport
11h15–12h15	histoire	anglais		musique	informatique	sport
			déjeuner			
13h45–14h45	sciences	dessin		anglais	français	
14h45–15h45	sport	sciences		histoire / géo	français	
			récréation			
16h–17h	sport			français		

par cœur

Learn this by heart.

Sophie déteste la géographie,
Clémence aime les sciences,
Grégoire aime l'histoire,
et Nestor adore le sport!

quarante-trois

l'école

- Say '**soixante**' as if the 'x' is a double 's'.

- Say '**quarante**' and '**cinquante**' as if the 'qu' is a 'k'.

19 récréation

Follow the numbers in the maze
in order to go from the entrance to the exit safely.

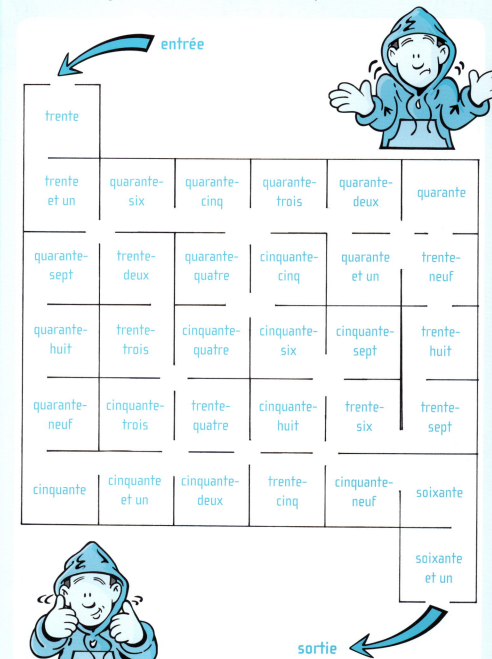

entrée

trente					
trente et un	quarante-six	quarante-cinq	quarante-trois	quarante-deux	quarante
quarante-sept	trente-deux	quarante-quatre	cinquante-cinq	quarante et un	trente-neuf
quarante-huit	trente-trois	cinquante-quatre	cinquante-six	cinquante-sept	trente-huit
quarante-neuf	cinquante-trois	trente-quatre	cinquante-huit	trente-six	trente-sept
cinquante	cinquante et un	cinquante-deux	trente-cinq	cinquante-neuf	soixante
					soixante et un

sortie

quarante-quatre

pour chanter

You can sing this to the tune of 'Frère Jacques'.

Lun-	di	ma-	tin
Mar-	di	ma-	tin
Jeu-	di	ma-	tin

J'ai	his-	toire
J'ai	mu-	sique
J'ai	fran-	çais

J'aime l'é-cole, j'aime l'his-toire
J'aime le prof de mu- sique
Ma ma-tière pré- fé- rée

C'est	su-	per!
Il est	sym-	pa!
C'est	gé-	nial!

Lundi matin,
Lundi matin,
J'ai histoire,
J'ai histoire.
J'aime l'école, j'aime l'histoire,
J'aime l'école, j'aime l'histoire.
C'est super!
C'est super!

Mardi matin,
Mardi matin,
J'ai musique,
J'ai musique.
J'aime le prof de musique,
J'aime le prof de musique.
Il est sympa!
Il est sympa!

Jeudi matin,
Jeudi matin,
J'ai français,
J'ai français,
Ma matière préférée,
Ma matière préférée.
C'est génial!
C'est génial!

mini-dico

trente et un	31
trente-deux	32
trente-trois	33
trente-quatre	34
trente-cinq	35
trente-six	36
trente-sept	37
trente-huit	38
trente-neuf	39
quarante	40
quarante et un	41
quarante-deux	42
quarante-trois	43
quarante-quatre	44
quarante-cinq	45
quarante-six	46
quarante-sept	47
quarante-huit	48
quarante-neuf	49
cinquante	50
cinquante et un	51
cinquante-deux	52
cinquante-trois	53
cinquante-quatre	54
cinquante-cinq	55
cinquante-six	56
cinquante-sept	57
cinquante-huit	58
cinquante-neuf	59
soixante	60
soixante et un	61
soixante-deux	62
soixante-trois	63
soixante-quatre	64
soixante-cinq	65
soixante-six	66
soixante-sept	67
soixante-huit	68
soixante-neuf	69

quarante-cinq

l'école

bons points

- To ask what the time is, you can either say '**il est quelle heure?**' or '**quelle heure est-il?**', which is more formal.

- Do not pronounce the 't' at the end of '**minuit**'.

- Pronounce the 'x' of '**deux**' as if it is a 'z' and run the two words ('**deux**' and '**heures**') together. Do the same with '**six heures**'.

- Pronounce the 's' of '**trois**' as if it is a 'z' and run the two words ('**trois**' and '**heures**') together.

- Pronounce the 'f' of '**neuf**' as if it is a 'v' and run the two words ('**neuf**' and '**heures**') together.

- Do not pronounce the 't' at the end of '**quart**', but don't forget the 'r'.

20 il est quelle heure?

Choose the right caption for each picture and add the time to each clock.

1 a Il est midi. ☐
  b Il est minuit. ☐

2 a Il est une heure et demie. ☐
  b Il est neuf heures moins le quart. ☐

3 a Il est onze heures et quart. ☐
  b Il est sept heures moins le quart. ☐

4 a Il est midi et demi. ☐
  b Il est trois heures et quart. ☐

5 a Il est cinq heures. ☐
  b Il est onze heures et demie. ☐

6 a Il est deux heures. ☐
  b Il est six heures et demie. ☐

mots croisés

Horizontalement ▶

1 il est 12 heures = il est _ _ _ _

6 il est 24 heures = il est _ _ _ _ _ _

7 il est trois _ _ _ _ _ _ et demie

10 il est 19 heures = il est _ _ _ _ heures

Verticalement ▼

2 il est 12 heures 30 = il est midi et _ _ _ _

3 il est 13 heures 15 = il est une heure et _ _ _ _ _ _

4 il est 20 heures 15 = il est huit heures _ _ quart

5 il est 20 heures 45 = il est neuf heures _ _ _ _ _ _ le quart

8 il _ _ _ minuit et demi

9 il est 18 heures = il est _ _ _ _ heures

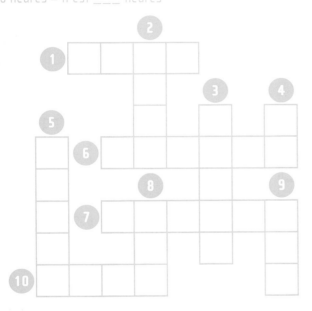

l'heure	time, o'clock
il est	it is
quelle heure?	what time?
midi	twelve (midday)
minuit	twelve (midnight)
et demi(e)	half past
et quart	quarter past
moins le quart	quarter to

par cœur

Learn this by heart.

Il est midi à Paris,
Neuf heures à Honfleur,
Quatre heures et quart à Colmar,
mais quelle heure est-il à Lille?

bons points

- Use 'à pied' to say you go on foot.

- Use 'à vélo' to say you cycle.

- Most other means of transport are introduced with 'en' – 'en bus', 'en train', 'en avion'.

21 à pied ou à vélo

Which means of transport are illustrated in this picture?

à vélo ❏
à pied ❏
en bus ❏
en train ❏
en avion ❏
en métro ❏
en bateau ❏
en voiture ❏
en tramway ❏

moi... moi... moi...

Complete the speech bubble saying how you and your friend go to school, and stick in a picture to illustrate it.

mini-dico

l'avion	aeroplane
le bateau	boat
le bus	bus
le train	train
le tramway	tram
le vélo	bicycle
la voiture	car
à pied	on foot
en bus	by bus

> Je vais à l'école ....
> Mon copain/Ma copine .... va à l'école ....
> ....

par cœur

When you have completed the speech bubble, learn it by heart.

Je vais à l'école ...

bons points

- Pronounce '**mon anniversaire**' as if '**anniversaire**' starts with an 'n'. It is the same for '**bon anniversaire**'.

- In French, '**anniversaire**' can mean either 'birthday' or 'anniversary'.

- Say '**quand**' as if it is spelt 'kan' – do not pronounce the 'u' nor the 'd' at the end.

22 bon anniversaire

Find in the grid the French for:

January	....	July	....
February	....	August	....
March	....	September	....
April	....	October	....
May	....	November	....
June	....	December	....

●	D	É	C	E	M	B	R	E	S
●	J	A	N	V	I	E	R	N	E
F	É	V	R	I	E	R	J	O	P
A	A	M	J	B	O	M	U	V	T
V	O	N	A	U	A	A	I	E	E
R	Û	N	N	R	I	I	L	M	M
I	T	I	V	E	S	N	L	B	B
L	R	S	A	I	R	E	E	R	R
O	C	T	O	B	R	E	T	E	E

The remaining letters make up a message. What is it?

....

moi... moi... moi...

Complete the speech bubbles with details of your birthday and that of your relatives or friends.
Add an illustration.

C'est quand, ton anniversaire?

Mon ....,
c'est le
....

C'est quand, l'anniversaire de ta maman/sœur/copine?

L'anniversaire de ma
............................,
c'est le
....

C'est quand, l'anniversaire de ton papa/copain/frère?

L'anniversaire de mon
............................,
c'est le
....

par cœur

When you have completed the bubbles, learn them by heart.

mini-dico

l'année	year
l'anniversaire	birthday
janvier	January
février	February
mars	March
avril	April
mai	May
juin	June
juillet	July
août	August
septembre	September
octobre	October
novembre	November
décembre	December
bon anniversaire	happy birthday
quand?	when?

l'année

bons points

- '**Il fait**' means literally 'it does'. It is used to introduce many weather expressions, such as '**il fait froid**' (it is cold) and '**il fait chaud**' (it is warm).

- Do not pronounce the 'd' at the end of '**froid**' and '**chaud**'. It is the same for '**brouillard**'.

- '**Il pleut**' can mean either 'it rains' or 'it is raining'. It is the same for '**il neige**'.

- Do not pronounce the 't' at the end of '**pleut**'. It is the same for '**vent**'.

23 il fait quel temps?

Are you an optimist? Try this quiz and find out...

En automne, il y a du vent...
■ ... et du brouillard. Je déteste l'automne.
● J'adore le vent. C'est marrant!

En hiver, il fait froid...
■ ... très froid. Je déteste l'hiver.
● ... et il neige! J'adore la neige. Super!

Au printemps, il fait moins froid...
● ... et il y a du soleil et des fleurs. C'est génial!
■ ... et il pleut. Je déteste la pluie.

En été, il y a du soleil. Il fait beau temps...
● ... et il fait chaud. C'est les vacances. J'adore l'été.
■ ... et il fait chaud... trop chaud. Je déteste l'été.

* dans la moyenne = average

Tu as 3 ou 4 ● : tu es optimiste. Super!
Tu as 2 ● : tu es dans la moyenne*...
Tu as 3 ou 4 ■ : tu es pessimiste! Oh, là, là...

mots croisés

Horizontalement ▶

4 il neige: il fait _____
5 il _____ beau temps
6 au printemps, il _____
7 en automne, il y a du
_____
10 en ____, il fait chaud
11 en hiver, il _____
12 Il fait quel _____?

Verticalement ▼

1 en été, il fait _____
2 il y a du _____: il fait chaud
3 en _____, il fait froid
6 au _____, il fait moins
froid
8 en _____, il y a du brouillard
9 en automne, il y a du brouillard et
du _____

mini-dico

l'automne	autumn
le brouillard	fog
l'été	summer
la fleur	flower
l'hiver	winter
le printemps	spring
le soleil	sun
le temps	weather
le vent	wind
beau	beautiful
chaud	hot, warm
froid	cold
moins	less
très	very
trop	too
en/au	in
il fait...	it is...
il neige	it snows/ is snowing
il pleut	it rains/ is raining
quel?	what?

par cœur

Learn this by heart.

Au printemps,
Gaétan
Aime les gants blancs.
Mais l'hiver,
Il préfère
Les pull-overs
Verts!

bons points

- The French for 70 is literally 'sixty-ten', 71 is 'sixty-eleven', and so on.

- The French for 80 is literally 'four-twenty', 81 is 'four-twenty-one', and so on.

- The French for 90 is literally 'eighty-ten', 91 is 'eighty-eleven', and so on.

24 récréation

Put the pairs back together.

90	quatre-vingt-un
76	quatre-vingt-dix-huit
80	soixante et onze
72	quatre-vingt-sept
95	soixante-treize
73	quatre-vingt-quatorze
97	soixante-quatorze
88	soixante-seize
74	quatre-vingt-dix
94	soixante-dix
75	quatre-vingt-seize
93	soixante-dix-sept
89	quatre-vingt-onze
77	quatre-vingt-douze
87	soixante-dix-huit
96	soixante-dix-neuf
71	quatre-vingt(s)
84	soixante-quinze
99	quatre-vingt-neuf
78	quatre-vingt-quinze
91	quatre-vingt-six
79	quatre-vingt-deux
81	quatre-vingt-trois
70	cent
82	quatre-vingt-quatre
92	quatre-vingt-cinq
83	quatre-vingt-huit
85	quatre-vingt-treize
100	quatre-vingt-dix-sept
86	quatre-vingt-dix-neuf
98	soixante-douze

cinquante-quatre

pour chanter

This song is popular with French children at Christmas time.
It is sung to the tune of 'Jingle Bells'.

Vive le vent, vive le vent
Vive le vent d'hiver
Qui s'en va sifflant, soufflant
Dans les grands sapins verts.
Vive le temps, vive le temps
Vive le temps d'hiver
Boules de neige et jour de l'an
Et bonne année grand-mère.

l'année

bons points

- All the boxes in colour represent days that are public holidays in France – there are 11 altogether.

- In France public holidays do not necessarily fall on a Monday.

- Good Friday is not a holiday in France.

- Boxing Day is not a holiday in France.

25 les jours de fête

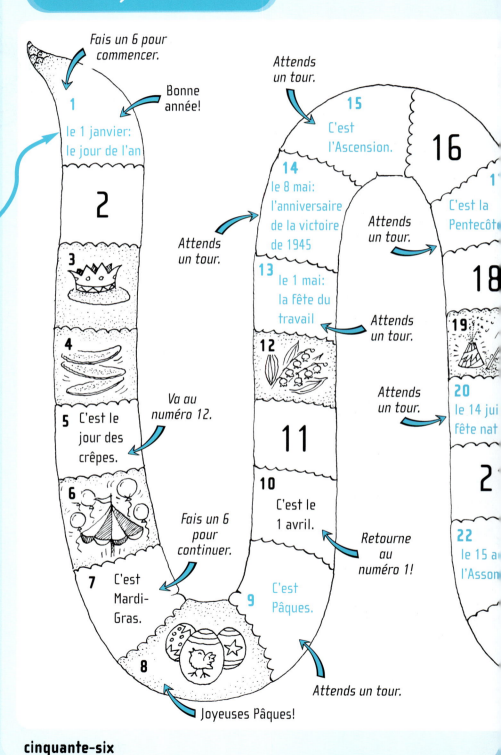

Fais un 6 pour commencer.

Bonne année!

1 le 1 janvier: le jour de l'an

2

3

4

5 C'est le jour des crêpes.

6

7 C'est Mardi-Gras.

8

Joyeuses Pâques!

Va au numéro 12.

Fais un 6 pour continuer.

9 C'est Pâques.

10 C'est le 1 avril.

11

12

13 le 1 mai: la fête du travail

14 le 8 mai: l'anniversaire de la victoire de 1945

15 C'est l'Ascension.

16

Attends un tour.

Attends un tour.

Attends un tour.

Attends un tour.

Attends un tour.

Retourne au numéro 1!

Attends un tour.

1' C'est la Pentecôte

18

19

20 le 14 jui fête nat

2

22 le 15 a l'Asson

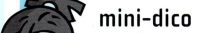
mini-dico

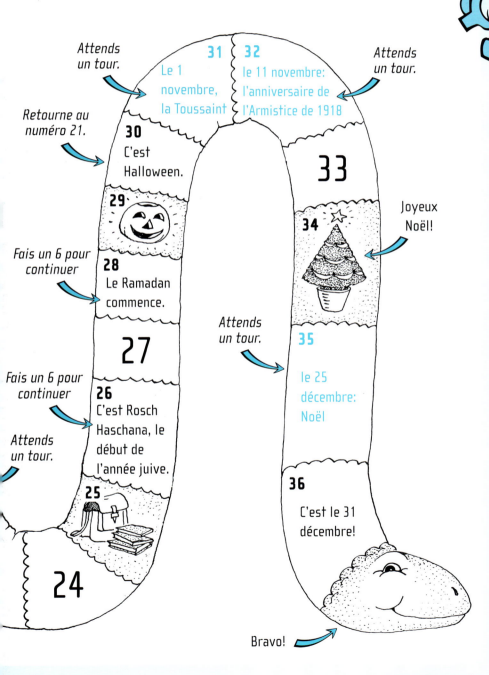

Attends un tour.

31 Le 1 novembre, la Toussaint

32 le 11 novembre: l'anniversaire de l'Armistice de 1918

Attends un tour.

Retourne au numéro 21.

30 C'est Halloween.

33

29

34

Joyeux Noël!

Fais un 6 pour continuer

28 Le Ramadan commence.

Fais un 6 pour continuer

27

Attends un tour.

35 le 25 décembre: Noël

Fais un 6 pour continuer

26 C'est Rosch Haschana, le début de l'année juive.

Attends un tour.

25

36 C'est le 31 décembre!

24

Bravo!

la crêpe	pancake
le début	beginning
la fête	holiday, festival
le jour	day
Noël	Christmas
Pâques	Easter
la Pentecôte	Whitsun
le travail	work, labour
la victoire	victory
juif/juive	Jewish
bonne année	happy new year
joyeuses Pâques	happy Easter
joyeux Noël	merry Christmas
attends un tour	miss a turn
fais un 6	throw a 6
pour commencer	to start
pour continuer	to continue
retourne	go back

réponses

présentations

1 salut!

- 1 salut, 2 oui, 3 non, 4 au secours, 5 merci, 6 ça va?, 7 ça va, 8 et toi?
- 1 salut!, 2 merci, 3 au secours!, 4 ça va?

2 au revoir!

- 1 au revoir, 2 bonsoir, 3 bonjour, 4 bonne nuit, 5 s'il te plaît

3 les numéros

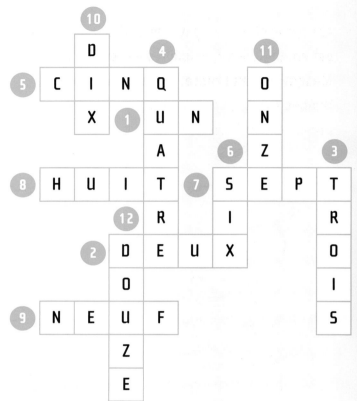

- 2 – Matthieu, 3 – François, six – Alice, 7- Annette, 9 – Monsieur Lebœuf, 12 – Madame Ventouse
- Milou is playing the guitar.

4 tu t'appelles comment?

- 1 Tu as quel âge?, 2 Tu t'appelles comment?, 3 Je m'appelle...
- Alex is the youngest (10); Sam is the oldest (12).

chez moi

5 tu habites où?

- Aberystwyth est au pays de Galles, Birmingham est en Angleterre, Bruxelles est en Belgique, Glasgow est en Ecosse, Chicago est aux USA, Québec est au Canada, Genève est en Suisse, Dublin est en Irlande, Paris est en France

Crossword:

```
                                    1
                                    G
            4              2  U  S  A
3  E  C  O  S  S  E                 L
      5        U                    L
      B  6  I  R  L  A  N  D  E     E
7     E        S           8        S
P     L        S           F
9 A  N  G  L  E  T  E  R  R  E
  Y   I                    A
  S   Q      10 C  A  N  A  D  A
      U                    C
      E                    E
```

6 ma maison

- 1 vrai, 2 vrai, 3 faux, 4 faux, 5 faux, 6 faux
- 1 chambre, 2 jardin, 3 maison, 4 cuisine, 5 salon, 6 escalier, 7 toilettes

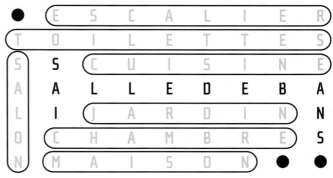

- salle de bains

7 ma famille

- 1 frère, 2 sœur, 3 père, 4 mère, 5 grand-père, 6 grand-mère, 7 beau-père, 8 belle-mère, 9 demi-sœur
- B

8 mes animaux

- 1 oui, 2 non, 3 oui, 4 non, 5 oui, 6 oui, 7 oui, 8 oui, 9 non, 10 oui

j'aime

9 bon appétit!

- A sandwich au poulet, B sandwich au jambon, C pizza aux champignons, D eau minérale, E sandwich au fromage, F limonade, G glace à la fraise, H salade, I glace à la vanille, J gâteau au chocolat, K frites, L jus d'orange

réponses

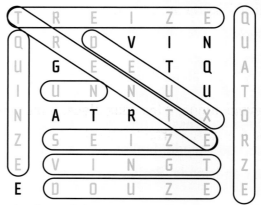

- vingt-quatre
- 1 vingt-cinq, 2 vingt-deux, 3 trente, 4 treize, 5 vingt, 6 dix-neuf

13 mes passe-temps

- 1 jouer aux cartes, 2 les ordinateurs, 3 lire, 4 danser, 5 j'aime ça, 6 je déteste ça

le look

14 mes couleurs préférées

- les couleurs primaires: red, yellow, blue
  les couleurs complémentaires: red and green, yellow and purple, blue and orange

15 le corps

- 1 les yeux, 2 les pieds, 3 les cheveux, 4 les bras, 5 le nez, 6 la tête, 7 le corps, 8 la bouche

16 mes vêtements préférés

- 1 le pantalon, 2 la veste, 3 les chaussures, 4 la cravate

10 mes copains

- A Hamid, B Julie, C `Matthieu, D Karima, E Océane, F Luc

11 le sport

- 1 j'aime l'équitation, 2 j'aime la planche à voile, 3 j'aime le basket, 4 j'aime le vélo

12 récréation

- treize, un, seize, vingt, douze, quinze, quatorze, deux, trente

- He is wearing a blue winter coat, grey jeans, brown (high) boots, a red hat, a green scarf and black gloves.

17 petit ou grand?

- 1 les cheveux longs, 2 les yeux bleus, 3 les yeux marrons, 4 mince, 5 grand, 6 petit

18 mes matières préférées

- lundi, mardi, mercredi, jeudi, vendredi, samedi, dimanche
- sport: b, maths: c, anglais: f, français: g, histoire: h, sciences: e, musique: d, géographie: i, informatique: a
- Samia's timetable

19 récréation

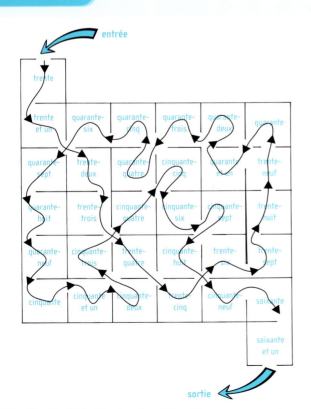

20 il est quelle heure?

- 1b, 2a, 3a, 4a, 5a, 6b.

réponses

21 à pied ou à vélo

- à vélo, à pied, en bus, en train, en avion, en bateau, en voiture

l'année

22 bon anniversaire

- janvier, février, mars, avril, mai, juin, juillet, août, septembre, octobre, novembre, décembre

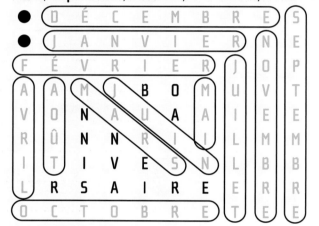

bon anniversaire

23 il fait quel temps?

24 récréation

90	quatre-vingt-dix
76	soixante-seize
80	quatre-vingts
72	soixante-douze
95	quatre-vingt-quinze
73	soixante-treize
97	quatre-vingt-dix-sept
88	quatre-vingt-huit
74	soixante-quatorze
94	quatre-vingt-quatorze
75	soixante-quinze
93	quatre-vingt-treize
89	quatre-vingt-neuf
77	soixante-dix-sept
87	quatre-vingt-sept
96	quatre-vingt-seize
71	soixante et onze
84	quatre-vingt-quatre
99	quatre-vingt-dix-neuf
78	soixante-dix-huit
91	quatre-vingt-onze
79	soixante-dix-neuf
81	quatre-vingt-un
70	soixante-dix
82	quatre-vingt-deux
92	quatre-vingt-douze
83	quatre-vingt-trois
85	quatre-vingt-cinq
100	cent
86	quatre-vingt-six
98	quatre-vingt-dix-huit

Timetable

	Lundi	Mardi	Mercredi	Jeudi	Vendredi

RÉCRÉATION

DÉJEUNER

RÉCRÉATION

Notes

soixante-quatre